Ooey-Gooey Animals

Leeches

Lola M. Schaefer

Heinemann Library
Chicago, Illinois

© 2002 Reed Educational & Professional Publishing
Published by Heinemann Library,
an imprint of Reed Educational & Professional Publishing,
Chicago, Illinois

Customer Service 888-454-2279
Visit our website at www.heinemannlibrary.com

Designed by Suzanne Emerson/Heinemann Library and Ginkgo Creative, Inc.
Printed and bound in the U.S.A. by Lake Book

06 05 04 03 02
10 9 8 7 6 5 4 3 2 1

Library of Congress Cataloging-in-Publication Data
Schaefer, Lola M., 1950-
    Leeches / Lola Schaefer.
        p. cm. — (Ooey-gooey animals)
Includes index.
Summary: Provides a basic introduction to leeches, including their habitat, diet, and physical features.
    ISBN 1-58810-506-7 (HC), 1-58810-715-9 (Pbk.)
    1. Leeches—Juvenile literature. [1. Leeches.] I. Title.
    QL391.A6 S33 2002
    592'.66—dc21

                                    2001003022

Acknowledgments
The author and publishers are grateful to the following for permission to reproduce copyright material:
Title page, pp. 9, 22 Gallo Images/Corbis; p. 4 Lester V. Bergman/Corbis; p. 5 Kevin Schafer/Corbis; p. 6 John D. Cunningham/Visuals Unlimited; p. 7 Robert Mitchell; p. 8 Glenn Oliver/Visuals Unlimited; p. 10 Bill Beatty/Visuals Unlimited; pp. 11, 13 John D. Cunningham/Visuals Unlimited; p. 12 Richard P. Smith; p. 14 David Liebman; p. 15 Dr. Darlyne Murawski/National Geographic Society; p. 16 Papilio/Corbis; p. 17 G. C. Lockwood/Bruce Coleman Inc.; pp. 18, 19 Jane Burton/Bruce Coleman Inc.; p. 20 R. Calentine/Visuals Unlimited; p. 21 Visuals Unlimited

Cover photograph courtesy of John D. Cunningham/Visuals Unlimited

Special thanks to our advisory panel for their help in the preparation of this book:

Eileen Day, Preschool Teacher
Chicago, IL

Paula Fischer, K–1 Teacher
Indianapolis, IN

Sandra Gilbert,
Library Media Specialist
Houston, TX

Angela Leeper,
Educational Consultant
North Carolina Department
of Public Instruction
Raleigh, NC

Pam McDonald,
Reading Teacher
Winter Springs, FL

Melinda Murphy,
Library Media Specialist
Houston, TX

Helen Rosenberg, MLS
Chicago, IL

Anna Marie Varakin,
Reading Instructor
Western Maryland College

Some words are shown in bold, **like this.**
You can find them in the picture glossary on page 23.

Contents

What Are Leeches?

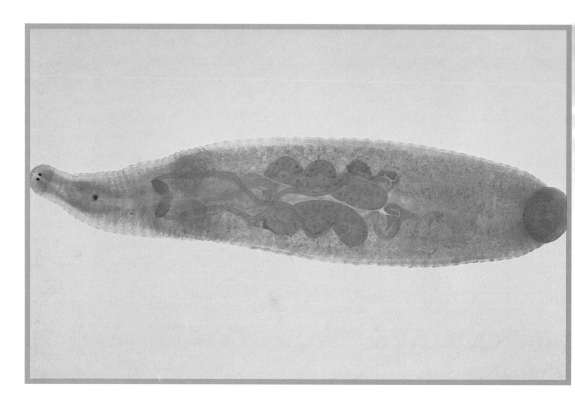

Leeches are animals without bones.

They are **invertebrates**.

Most leeches are short and thin.

Where Do Leeches Live?

Most leeches live in lakes or ponds.

Some leeches live in oceans.

Land leeches live on plants in warm, wet places.

What Do Leeches Look Like?

Leeches look like flat worms.

They can be tan, black, or red.

sucker

sucker

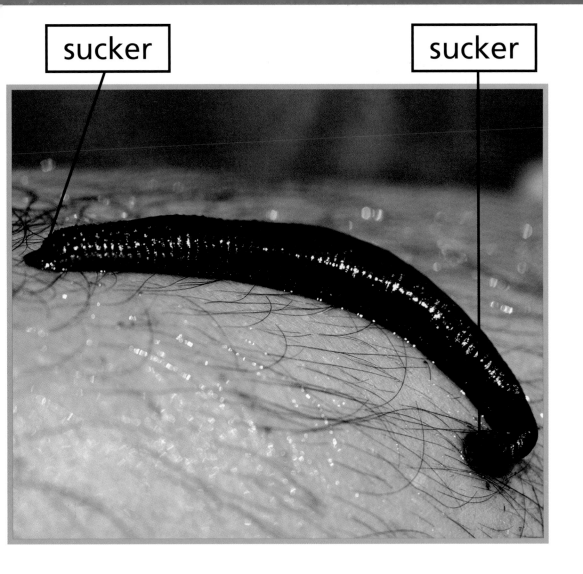

Leeches have a **sucker** under each end of their bodies.

Suckers help leeches hold on to things.

What Do Leeches Feel Like?

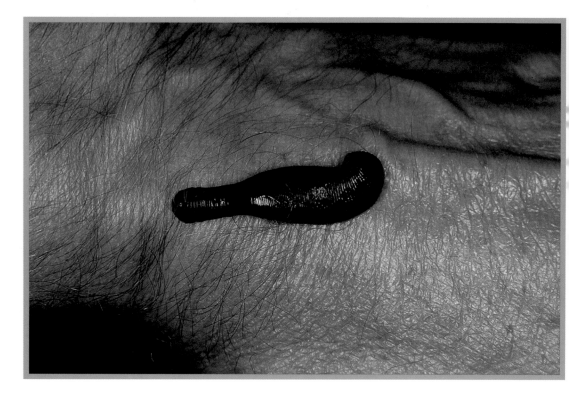

Leeches feel gooey.

Mucus covers their smooth bodies.

mucus

Mucus helps keep leeches from drying out.

How Big Are Leeches?

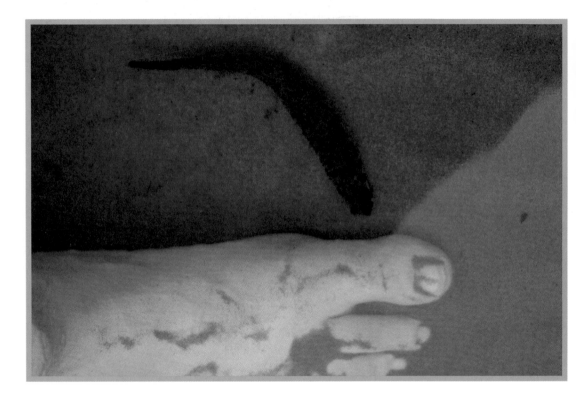

Leeches can be as short as an eyelash.

Some leeches are almost as long as a man's foot.

Before they eat, leeches are
as wide as your little finger.

After they eat, leeches are
much bigger.

How Do Leeches Move?

In water, leeches swim.

They wiggle their bodies from side to side.

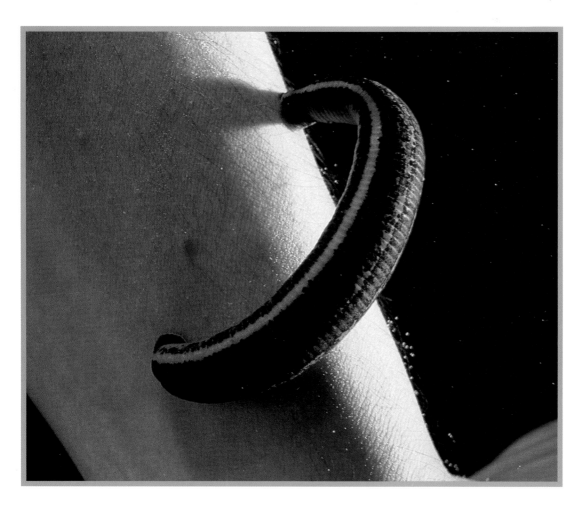

On land, leeches put down one **sucker**.

Then, they can pull their bodies
up or down.

What Do Leeches Eat?

worm

Many leeches eat worms and snails.

Leeches eat young bugs, too.

leeches

Land leeches bite larger animals.

They suck their blood for food.

What Do Leeches Do?

fish   sucker

Leeches wait for an animal to come near.

Then, they bite the animal to suck its blood.

They let go when they are
finished eating.

Where Do New Leeches Come From?

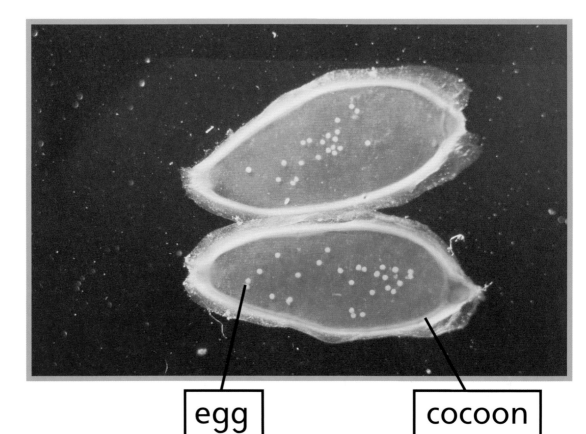

egg   cocoon

All adult leeches lay eggs in
a **cocoon.**

Water leeches put their cocoons
on underwater plants or rocks.

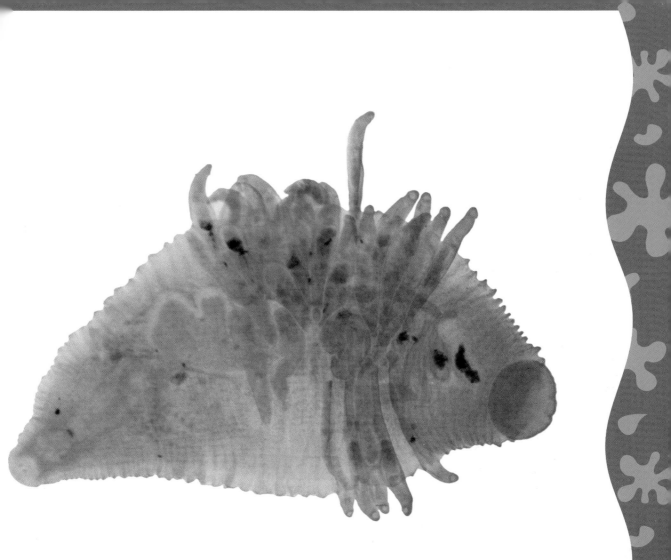

Land leeches put their cocoons in wet dirt.

Little leeches come out of the eggs.

Quiz

What are these leech parts?

Can you find them in the book?

Look for the answers on page 24.

?

?

?

Picture Glossary

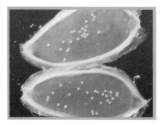

cocoon
(kuh-KOON)
pages 20, 21

invertebrate
(in-VUR-tuh-brate)
page 4

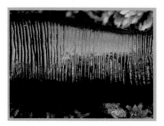

mucus
(MYOO-kus)
pages 10, 11

sucker
pages 9, 15, 18

Note to Parents and Teachers

Reading for information is an important part of a child's literacy development. Learning begins with a question about something. Help children think of themselves as investigators and researchers by encouraging their questions about the world around them. Each chapter in this book begins with a question. Read the question together. Look at the pictures. Talk about what you think the answer might be. Then read the text to find out if your predictions were correct. Think of other questions you could ask about the topic, and discuss where you might find the answers. Assist children in using the picture glossary and the index to practice new vocabulary and research skills.

! CAUTION: Remind children that it is not a good idea to handle wild animals. Children should wash their hands with soap and water after they touch any animal.

Index

Answers to quiz on page 22

sucker

mucus

sucker